Gulf of Mexico

Straits of Florida

Florida Bay

Canaveral Nat'l Seashore
Mosquito Lagoon
John F. Kennedy Space Center
Merritt Island
Melbourne
Sebastian
Gifford
Vero Beach
Fort Pierce
Port St. Lucie
Stuart
Port Salerno
West Palm Beach
Lake Worth
Boynton Beach
Delray Beach
Boca Raton
Pompano Beach
Fort Lauderdale
Plantation
Hialeah
Miami
Coral Gables
Bisca... Nat'l
Key Largo
Homestead

Titusville
Deltona
Sanford
Orlando
Winter Garden
Leesburg
Inverness
Brooksville
Spring Hill
Dade City
Walt Disney World
Kissimmee
St. Cloud
Lakeland
Brandon
Tampa
Dunedin
Clearwater
Largo
Pinellas Park
St. Petersburg
Bradenton
Sarasota
Venice
Port Charlotte
Punta Gorda
Fort Myers
Cape Coral
Naples
Marco
Captiva I.
Sanibel I.
Charlotte Harbor
Port Charlotte

95
75
27
4
75

Florida's Turnpike
Kissimmee R.
Lake Okeechobee
Lake Kissimmee
Peace R.
Caloosahatchee R.
Tampa Bay

Big Cypress National Preserve
Everglades Nat'l Park

Key West

Hemingway House

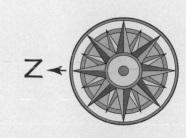

N

0   20   40   60   80

Distance in miles

CAROL M. HIGHSMITH AND TED LANDPHAIR

FLORIDA
A PHOTOGRAPHIC TOUR

CRESCENT BOOKS

NEW YORK

CAD CC MAX

FRONT COVER: Even in neighborhoods that have been extensively restored, like South Beach's Art Deco district in Miami Beach, Florida retains a casual feel. BACK COVER: Wading flamingos, such as these at Miami's Metrozoo, are a colorful Florida attraction. Wild flamingos, herons, egrets, and parrots also frequent back-yards and canals. PAGE 1: It was the allure of Florida's incredible beaches that convinced entre-preneurs to push development south-ward along the coasts. Here, the "Sunshine State" earned its nickname. PAGES 2–3: It's easy to see why Broward County is called the "Venice of Florida." Singer Barbara Mandrell lives along one of the canals that connect Fort Lauderdale with its spectacular beach.

This 1998 edition is published by Crescent Books,
an imprint of Random House Value Publishing,
a division of Random House, Inc., New York.

Crescent is a registered trademark and the colophon
is a trademark of Random House, Inc.

Random House
New York • Toronto • London • Sydney • Auckland
www.randomhouse.com

Printed and bound in China

Library of Congress Cataloging-in-Publication
Data
Highsmith, Carol M., 1946–
Florida /
Carol M. Highsmith and Ted Landphair.
p.   cm. — (A photographic tour)
Includes index.
ISBN 0-517-18613-6 (hc: alk. paper)
1. Florida—Pictorial works. I. Landphair,
Ted, 1942— . II. Title. III. Series: Highsmith,
Carol M., 1946— Photographic tour.
F312.H54   1997   97-19778
975.9—dc21   CIP

8 7 6 5 4 3 2

Project Editor: Donna Lee Lurker
Production Supervisor: Michael Siebert
Designed by Robert L. Wiser, Archetype Press, Inc.,
Washington, D.C.

All photographs by Carol M. Highsmith
unless otherwise credited:
map by XNR Productions, page 5; The John and
Mable Ringling Museum, Sarasota, page 6;
Library of Congress, Prints and Photographs
Division, pages 8–9, 13, 15, 20; The Henry
Morrison Flagler Museum, Palm Beach,
pages 10–11; NASA, page 12; Flagler College,
Saint Augustine, page 14; Ybor City State
Museum, Tampa, pages 16–17;
Edison-Ford Winter Estates, Fort Myers,
pages 18–19; The Orlando Sentinel, page 21

THE AUTHORS GRATEFULLY ACKNOWLEDGE
THE SUPPORT PROVIDED BY

HILTON HOTELS CORPORATION

AND

THE KEY WEST HILTON RESORT
AND MARINA

THE MIAMI AIRPORT HILTON
AND TOWERS

THE PALM BEACH AIRPORT HILTON

THE SAINT PETERSBURG
BAYFRONT HILTON

IN CONNECTION WITH THE COMPLETION
OF THIS BOOK

THE AUTHORS ALSO WISH TO THANK THE
FOLLOWING FOR THEIR GENEROUS
ASSISTANCE AND HOSPITALITY DURING
THEIR VISITS TO FLORIDA

The Ritz-Carlton, Amelia Island

The Riverside Hotel, Fort Lauderdale

Sanibel Harbour Resort & Spa, Fort Myers

The Sheraton Four Points, Lakeland

The Peabody, Orlando

The Best Western, Pensacola Beach

Florida Tourism Industry Marketing Corporation

Amelia Island and Historic Fernandina Beach
Visitors Bureau

Greater Fort Lauderdale
Convention & Visitors Bureau

Greater Miami Convention & Visitors Bureau

Tampa/Hillsborough Convention
and Visitors Association, Inc.

Travel South USA, Atlanta

Professor Cantor Brown, Tampa

Rosann G. Garcia
Customized Historic Tours & Events, Tampa

Marc and Rosemarie Kuhn, Plantation

Steve Mayberry, Enterprise Florida, Inc.

Bob McNeel Sr., Florida History Museum,
Tallahassee

Deborah Nordeen and Rick Cook,
Everglades National Park

Michelle Payer, Tampa

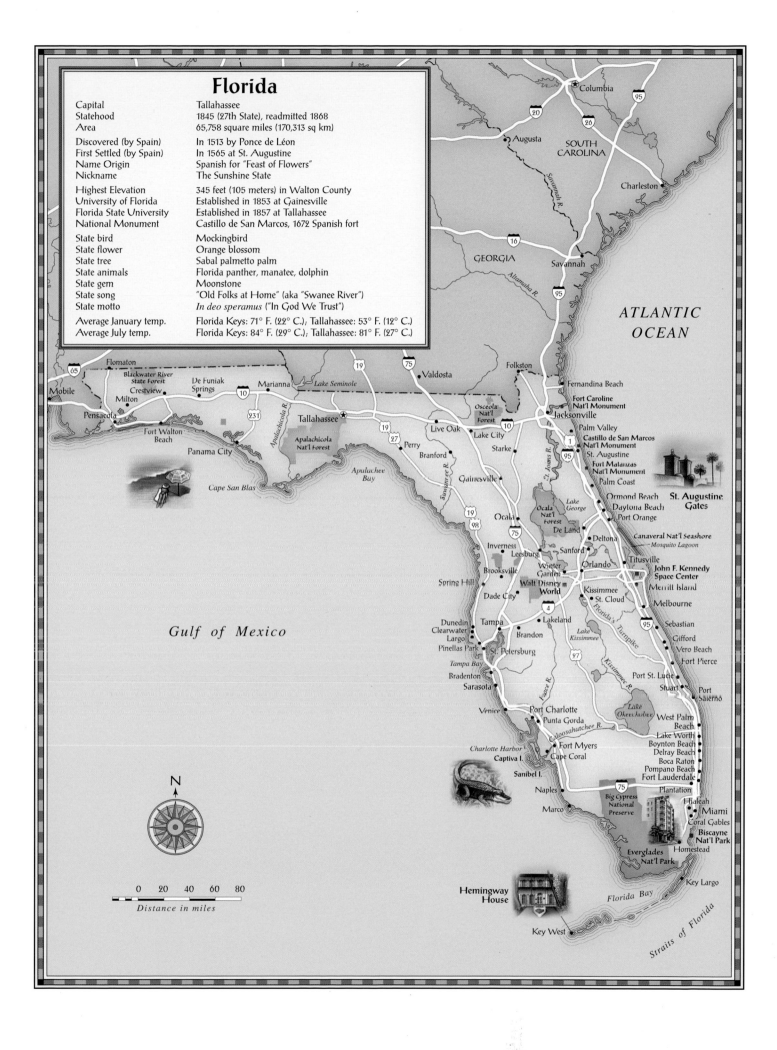

Florida

Capital	Tallahassee
Statehood	1845 (27th State), readmitted 1868
Area	65,758 square miles (170,313 sq km)
Discovered (by Spain)	In 1513 by Ponce de Léon
First Settled (by Spain)	In 1565 at St. Augustine
Name Origin	Spanish for "Feast of Flowers"
Nickname	The Sunshine State
Highest Elevation	345 feet (105 meters) in Walton County
University of Florida	Established in 1853 at Gainesville
Florida State University	Established in 1857 at Tallahassee
National Monument	Castillo de San Marcos, 1672 Spanish fort
State bird	Mockingbird
State flower	Orange blossom
State tree	Sabal palmetto palm
State animals	Florida panther, manatee, dolphin
State gem	Moonstone
State song	"Old Folks at Home" (aka "Swanee River")
State motto	*In deo speramus* ("In God We Trust")
Average January temp.	Florida Keys: 71° F. (22° C.); Tallahassee: 53° F. (12° C.)
Average July temp.	Florida Keys: 84° F. (29° C.); Tallahassee: 81° F. (27° C.)

SOUTH CAROLINA

Columbia

Augusta

Charleston

GEORGIA

ATLANTIC OCEAN

Savannah

Folkston

Valdosta

Fernandina Beach

Flomaton

Blackwater River State Forest

De Funiak Springs

Marianna

Lake Seminole

Fort Caroline Nat'l Monument

Mobile

Milton

Crestview

Jacksonville

Palm Valley

Pensacola

Fort Walton Beach

Tallahassee

Live Oak

Lake City

Osceola Nat'l Forest

Castillo de San Marcos Nat'l Monument

St. Augustine

Fort Matanzas Nat'l Monument

St. Augustine Gates

Panama City

Apalachicola Nat'l Forest

Perry

Branford

Starke

Gainesville

Palm Coast

Cape San Blas

Apaluchee Bay

Ocala

Ocala Nat'l Forest

Lake George

Ormond Beach

Daytona Beach

Port Orange

Gulf of Mexico

De Land

Inverness

Leesburg

Sanford

Deltona

Canaveral Nat'l Seashore

Mosquito Lagoon

Brooksville

Winter Garden

Orlando

Titusville

John F. Kennedy Space Center

Merritt Island

Spring Hill

Walt Disney World

Kissimmee

St. Cloud

Melbourne

Dade City

Lakeland

Florida's Turnpike

Sebastian

Dunedin

Clearwater

Largo

Tampa

Brandon

Lake Kissimmee

Gifford

Vero Beach

Pinellas Park

St. Petersburg

Fort Pierce

Tampa Bay

Port St. Lucie

Bradenton

Sarasota

Stuart

Port Salerno

Venice

Port Charlotte

Punta Gorda

Lake Okeechobee

West Palm Beach

Lake Worth

Charlotte Harbor

Captiva I.

Fort Myers

Cape Coral

Boynton Beach

Delray Beach

Boca Raton

Sanibel I.

Naples

Pompano Beach

Fort Lauderdale

Plantation

Big Cypress National Preserve

Hialeah

Miami

Marco

Coral Gables

Biscayne Nat'l Park

Everglades Nat'l Park

Homestead

Hemingway House

Key Largo

Florida Bay

Straits of Florida

Key West

N

0 20 40 60 80

Distance in miles

WHAT IS THE REAL FLORIDA? PARADISE? With its tropical enclaves of bobbing boats, exotic birds, pristine beaches, and manicured golf courses, it certainly fits that description. Even South Florida communities near the Atlantic Ocean and Gulf of Mexico are often cooler in summer than New York or Washington, D.C., and some winters, most of the state never sees sleet or snow. Breathtaking flowers, from orchids to blazing stars to flowering water hyacinths, thrive in Florida's hammocks and marshes. The Old South? Absolutely so in the northern counties, with their graceful homes, piney woods, and scent of magnolia. Urban America? More so than any other southern state; Florida has been a go-go place, growing by seven hundred to one thousand people a day, and sometimes more, since the 1970s. Rural? Its vast cattle ranches, citrus orchards, truck farms, cotton fields, and wide expanses of saw palmettos more than qualify. Multicultural? Absolutely; Florida was Spanish longer than it has been English or American, and the impact of Hispanic, African-American, Native American, and other cultures can be seen in every corner of the state. Sophisticated? Check out the lively street cafés on Fort Lauderdale's Las Olas Boulevard; Worth Avenue's swanky shops in Palm Beach, Jacksonville's vibrant waterfront, and world-class museums of art in Sarasota, DeLand, Gainesville, Miami, and Jacksonville to see just *how* stylish.

Fun? From its gigantic theme parks, seaquariums and serpentariums, jungle and bird gardens, battlefield sites, Indian mounds, and eccentric man-made attractions, it has long been America's playground. Sporting? No other state has all of these: pro and college football, basketball, and baseball; major-league hockey; horse and dog racing; championship tennis, golf, and auto racing; pro rodeos; and even polo. And at jai-alai arenas, the fifteenth-century Basque game, in which the *pelota* travels at upwards of 180 miles per hour, is played and wagered upon. Florida is a mecca for fishers—more than seven hundred species have been caught in Florida waters—and for hunters, water-skiers, jet-skiers, windsurfers, divers, hikers, skydivers, and even sponge divers. Even as early as the sixteenth century, Florida was identified as a place to relax and enjoy the outdoors: French painter Jacques Le Moyne de Morgues depicted the Timucua Indians swimming, boating, fishing, and otherwise frolicking in this natural fairyland. Florida is home to ten national parks, fifty state parks, three national forests, four state forests, and forty-three-hundred square miles of interior lakes and waterways. Progressive? Great missions into space launch in Florida; international corporations and banks are headquartered there; and both tourism and economic development have been taken out of the hands of government bureaucrats and placed under the watch of dynamic private-public partnerships.

Yet somehow, with all of its urbane development and cultural flamboyance, the Sunshine State is still wild and forbidding, from the Okefenokee Swamp in the far north to the Everglades, cypress preserves, and mangrove swamps of the far south. In Florida's considerable wilderness, alligators, crocodiles, four kinds of poisonous snakes, and plants whose sap can kill are not tourist attractions to be trifled with.

Hard as it is to imagine when admiring the pastels of Art Deco hotels along South Beach, across Biscayne Bay from Miami, or when dreamily casting for tarpon off the Lee Island Coast or riding the Skyway Express through downtown Jacksonville, Florida, like the Old West, was every bit the American frontier. Just a century ago, cattle were Florida's gold, phosphate was mined from the state's porous rock, oranges and rum were shipped from Saint Augustine as

J. H. Phillips created this elegant 1928 watercolor of the John and Mable Ringling Museum of Art in Sarasota. World travelers, the Ringlings furnished their museum, next to their Cà d'Zan mansion, with art treasures, especially Italian Baroque and Renaissance paintings. The State of Florida now owns the Ringling Museum.

Key West has always been a lusty town, appealing to artists, writers, brigands—and even a plain-speaking president, Harry S Truman, who established his Winter White House on the island.

early as the 1760s, Florida timber and tar supplied both Spanish and British navies, and North Florida became a stalwart center of the South's Cotton Kingdom. Three violent Seminole Indian rebellions—including the longest war in U.S. history—were fresh in the state's memory, and railroads had just pushed through the swamps into South Florida. At a time when New Orleans was the thriving Queen City of the South, and San Francisco's grand hotels hosted the nation's elite, Miami was a scrubby outpost of two hundred or so souls, scratching out a living raising coontee (a tuber used by Indians to make starch) and experimenting with sugar cultivation. So fearsome were mosquitoes from present-day Daytona Beach southward that one entrepreneur after another gave up trying to develop the beachfront, and throughout South Florida came documented reports of laborers driven crazy even trying.

Resorts? Eden? Hardly. The Florida Peninsula was a blistering-hot, insufferably humid, swampy and storm-lashed wasteland, so rife with yellow fever that even the Spanish did not bother to colonize in any numbers. It was a useful place for a few miserable military outposts that kept an eye on their silver trade from South America, gliding past on the Gulf Stream. Spanish explorer Juan Ponce de León, sailing from Puerto Rico, had first sighted the coast of Florida on March 27, 1513. He went ashore near the mouth of the Saint Johns River, claimed the new lands for Spain, and named them *Pascua florida* for the Easter celebration of the Feast of Flowers. Later stories of Ponce de León's searching for an elusive Fountain of Youth are tantalizing but almost certainly apocryphal. He was searching, all right, but for gold and natives to capture as slaves. Spanish missionaries later mounted missions into the interior to Christianize the Indians. And they did build a settlement at Saint Augustine, beginning in 1565, but only to stanch French incursions into Spanish territory; French Huguenots had moved onto Amelia Island and built Fort Caroline at the base of a bluff overlooking the Saint Johns River. The Spanish killed them all. Thus Spanish Saint Augustine ranks as the oldest permanent settlement in what would one day become the United States.

Though it bothered to explore only part of it, Spain considered its Florida colony to extend as far north as present-day North Carolina and as far west as the north shores of Louisiana's Lake Pontchartrain. This notion brought the Spanish into repeated conflicts with the colonial empires of Britain and France. Georgia Colony's royal governor, James Oglethorpe, repeatedly attacked Spanish settlements in North Florida, and in 1763, after Great Britain had seized Havana during the Seven Years' War, Spain was compelled to turn over all of Florida to the British in order to get Cuba back. But British governors had barely settled into the old Spanish capitals of East Florida at Saint Augustine and West Florida at Pensacola than they had to give the new territory back to Spain in 1783. It was a price for losing the American Revolution, in which Spain was an American ally. This Spanish hold on Florida was quickly threatened again, however, this time by rambunctious Americans, who had wantonly moved into many parts of Spanish domain. Soon after the Louisiana Purchase, Louisiana Territory kicked Spanish administrators out of the "Florida parishes," and in 1812 a motley collection of American, English, and Spanish planters, as well as Spanish army deserters, proclaimed the rest of West Florida an independent republic. Even though this was still Spanish territory, it was American general Andrew Jackson and his force of Tennessee frontiersmen who put an end to this rebellion on his way to New Orleans to battle the British at the end of the War of 1812. Afterward, Jackson would return to Florida to put down an Indian uprising, and by 1819 Spain was through bothering with its largely worthless Florida colony. In 1821 it simply gave it to the United States. Andrew Jackson briefly ran the government until William Duval took over as the first governor of the new U.S. Territory of Florida.

Alabama and Mississippi were soon carved out, and people in what was left of Florida set about building towns and establishing cotton, tobacco, and sugarcane plantations. All the while, white settlers mercilessly persecuted the indigenous Seminoles. Early historians translated the name to mean "renegades." They had been a branch of the Creek nation in Alabama and Georgia who migrated south into Florida and intermarried with other Native Americans, free blacks, and white fugitives. Many Florida Seminoles became wealthy raising cattle and selling them in Savannah and Saint Augustine. But in a long and bloody conflict after Florida Seminoles resisted President Jackson's order that Eastern tribes be forcibly removed to the new Indian Territory in Oklahoma, the Seminole population was reduced to a few hundred survivors hiding deep in the wretched Everglades.

Florida became the nation's twenty-seventh state in 1845, in time for the planter aristocracy to enthusiastically support slavery—slaves made up an amazing 45 percent of the state population in 1860—and support the calls for southern secession. Few Civil War battles were fought in its territory, however; Key West, home of the Union's Fort Taylor, kept watch over Union blockade vessels, and the Keys never had a chance to support the Rebel cause. But upstate, coastal inlets provided safe harbor to Confederate blockade runners, much as they had for notorious pirates like Black Caesar in previous decades. Following the war and a relatively peaceful Reconstruction period, conservative "Bourbon Democrats" took power in Tallahassee. It would be ninety years before a Republican would again occupy the governor's mansion. "Pork Chop Democrats," a *Tampa Tribune* editor later called the state's

By 1933, when this photograph of beach-front reverie was taken, sultry Miami and its beaches were secrets no longer. Even back then, the Goodyear blimp "Reliance" was flying tourists over the scene.

power brokers, were based in the northern counties and held tenaciously to power by suppressing the influence of urban communities until the U.S. Supreme Court directed legislatures nationwide to more fairly apportion lower-house seats according to population. The derisive "pork chop" term was a reference to the scattering of pig farms in North Florida; conversely, the higher and mightier of South Florida were said to be "lamb choppers," a reference to the preferred cuisine of wealthy Yankees who had settled there.

In 1880, all of Florida had a population of only 269,493. Fifty years later, that total had multiplied more than eighteen times. Later, migration to Florida became a virtual stampede. The population grew by 43 percent in the 1970s alone, and another 33 percent in the 1980s. Three men, Henry Flagler, Hamilton Disston, and Henry B. Plant, were largely responsible for opening the Florida Peninsula to settlement. Plant was a railroad man who extended his line from Georgia south to Orlando, then down past Kissimmee to the west coast in the 1880s, building great tourist hotels when he reached the Gulf. Disston, a Philadelphia industrialist, talked the governor into selling him four million acres of central Florida for twenty-five cents an acre. He drained even more acres near Lake Okeechobee and began subdividing.

Flagler, a New Yorker who was treasurer of John D. Rockefeller's Standard Oil Company and a director of Plant's railroad company, followed Plant's example on Florida's east coast. Saint Augustine was the end of civilization when millionaire Flagler took his second wife there for a winter's stay in 1885. Sleepy, tumble-down Saint Augustine had been an invalids' watering hole, what Flagler College history professor Thomas Graham later called "a macabre colony of people who were coughing, dying, and also playing the flute, because that was one way you could keep your lungs clear, by playing a wind instrument." Flagler himself went to Saint Augustine to recuperate from a liver ailment. He took note of a luxury wooden hotel, the San Marco, which had opened to "strangers," as locals called visitors. Flagler decided to build his own Xanadu on spongy land that held lemon and orange groves just outside the old Spanish defense perimeter. The result was a soaring concrete edifice with great twin towers, terra-cotta balconies, and red-tile roofs. Flagler named the hotel the "Ponce de León." Inside was a cascade of opulence: George Maynard murals, marble floors and fireplaces, Virgilio Tojetti canvasses, and carved-wood paneling. The eight-hundred-seat dining hall boasted an elliptical barrel-vault ceiling, Tiffany stained-glass windows, and musicians' galleries. Three years later he added a less haughty hotel, the Alcazar. Others put up similar palaces, and, seemingly overnight, Saint Augustine was transformed into America's "winter Newport." Soon, though, Flagler was off draining swamps and opening an entire resort community, Palm Beach, almost two hundred miles to the south. Here, Flagler erected not just the grand Breakers Hotel, but also fine homes, including a seventy-three-room mansion, Whitehall, for himself and his third wife. West Palm Beach, now the larger of the two Palm Beach cities, began as a neighborhood for the servants of Palm Beach's *haute monde*. For the rich, Florida was a backwater no longer.

Decent roads and the Model T Ford soon opened the state to average Americans as well. Some constructed makeshift campers and trailers to bring their families along for the ride. "Tin Can Tourists," the natives called them. They were the first "snowbirds"—visitors by the tens of thousands who migrated to Florida during the temperate

Florida East Coast Railroad and the luxury hotels founded by Gilded Age entrepreneur Henry Morrison Flagler, shown here with his wife, Mary, established tourism as Florida's economic foundation.

wintertime, then fled back north to escape the torpid summers. But not just balmy temperatures lured them to the Sunshine State. So did exotic attractions—hot springs and dancing waters, snake and alligator farms, horse tracks, and every imaginable variety of illegal but tolerated gambling, including slot machines and a Cuban numbers game called *bolita*.

Some Americans discovered the allure of Florida's climate and beaches at the turn of the century, when they shoved off to Cuba during the Spanish-American War. Others were stationed there during World War I. But it was World War II, during which two million service personnel trained for combat in Florida, that planted the seeds of the state's biggest population explosion. After the war, air-conditioning and rampant land speculation opened the floodgates to year-round, permanent in-migration. As the turn of the twenty-first century neared, Florida had grown from a drowsy subtropical hinterland into a cosmopolitan state. Suddenly exotic Florida, which had ranked thirty-third among states in population in 1900, twenty-sixth in 1940, and nineteenth in 1950, was the nation's fourth-largest state—the shooting star of the Sun Belt. Four-fifths of its people lived in towns and cities. Today in some rural Florida counties, a majority of residents reside in mobile homes, often in plush, gated surroundings. Millions of retirees moved to high-rise complexes in Florida's beach communities, increasing the tax base but also the demand for social services. Sometimes friction developed when elderly Floridians voted down increased spending for schools and other public services.

All the while, Florida never lost its Hispanic presence. The number of Spaniards and Latins was relatively small after Spain abandoned Florida in 1821, but after the Civil War expatriate Cubans began a thriving cigar-making trade, first in Key West, then in the Ybor City neighborhood of Tampa. In 1929, a fledgling commercial airline with the grandiose name "Pan

Henry Flagler built opulent Whitehall, on Cocoanut Row in Palm Beach, for his third wife, Mary, in 1901. Sold by heirs, it served as a luxury hotel until 1959 and is now a museum.

Apollo 11 lifts off from the Kennedy Space Center in Cape Canaveral in 1969. During the mission, astronauts Neil Armstrong and Edwin Aldrin took "one small step"—and more—on the moon.

American World Airways" made its inaugural flight to Havana from Key West, presaging regular service between Miami and the Cuban capital. A generation later, after the Cuban revolution of 1959, the culture of South Florida changed dramatically with the arrival, first of wealthy Cuban professionals and business leaders, then of ordinary Cubans fleeing by the boatload from Fidel Castro's Communist regime. They settled in Miami's "Little Havana," where to this day statues and memorials to Cuban resistance leaders abound, and Spanish signs, music, and language fill the streets and shops of the area. Much of Cuba's wealth was transferred to South Florida banks, and Miami became a financial, shipping, and transportation magnet for all of Latin America.

Unchecked growth in parts of Florida proved a formidable challenge, however. Attempts to slow development were met with Floridians' ingrained resentment of government control, dating to the frontier days. A casualty was Florida's once-unsullied environment. The proliferation of housing tracts and high-rise boulevards, man-made canals, and drainage projects began to erode beaches, denude woodlands, pollute rivers and lakes, and threaten some wildlife species nearly to the point of extinction. Thousands of acres of the Everglades alone were drained to create agricultural land or subdivisions. In desperation lest paradise be paved over by parking lots, Republican governor Claude Kirk Jr. and Democrats Reubin Askew and Bob Graham pushed through increasingly strict legislation to manage growth in the 1960s and '70s. They set aside green space, and barred developers from the doors of Florida's natural treasures. No more would a few con artists be allowed to stake out streets and sign up gullible buyers for fanciful swampland neighborhoods that never materialized.

Finding the revenue to fund these and other state government programs has been a thorny issue in Florida. Voters repeatedly reject suggestions that the state impose a personal income tax. And homeowners have held tight to their hefty homestead exemptions that cut into property-tax revenue. To compensate, Florida has taxed utilities, liquor, cigarettes, and gasoline at higher-than-average rates, and relied on the more than forty million tourists who visit annually to underwrite much of the state budget. Spending on education remained relatively low, even by southern standards, and student achievement reflected this inattention. Finally recognizing that it must improve its educational system to compete for high-tech jobs in the century to come, Florida began a massive upgrading of standards and spending in the 1990s, first in its community colleges, vocational programs, and state universities, and then in its secondary schools.

A wholesale restructuring of the state's economic-development apparatus began in 1989 with publication of a Florida Chamber of Commerce report called *Cornerstone*. It concluded that the underfunded state government alone could not keep the burgeoning state competitive. Eventually the legislature and governor agreed to abolish the state Department of Commerce and turn economic and tourism development over to separate business-government partnership corporations. The economic arm, Enterprise Florida, Incorporated (EFI), set about fostering entrepreneurship, capital growth, and job creation in order to attract high-paying aerospace, computer, and other high-tech businesses. It also helped spur creation of a venture-capital fund that reached $35 million by the mid-1990s, in an effort to "grow" new industries.

In many corners of Florida, beginning at the southernmost point of the continental United States in Key West, ninety miles from Cuba, that business is tourism. The Keys are a 110-mile-long necklace of islands tied by forty-five bridges to the mainland. Some keys are little more than landfill, built to accommodate U.S. 1, the only road to Key West, and separating the Atlantic Ocean and Gulf of Mexico by a hundred yards or so. Henry Flagler extended his railroad through the keys to Key West by 1912. That town, which retains the easygoing ambience of a tropical colonial capital, became a melting pot of Cuban, Bahamian, and Conch (white) cultures. The mix of wealthy and famous homeowners—including President Harry S Truman, who kept his Winter White House there—military personnel, and inveterate beach bums and drifters proved too intoxicating for writers to resist. Novelists, poets, and playwrights like Ernest Hemingway, Tennessee Williams, Marjorie Kinnan Rawlings, and Elizabeth Bishop lived and wrote prolifically there. Above Key West, the Middle Keys survive on fishing, diving, and snorkeling, while Upper Keys like Tavernier and Key Largo have largely become a bedroom community for South Dade County.

Miami was little more than a forlorn army outpost until 1884, when a large hotel, the Peacock Inn, opened in a section that became known as Coconut Grove. Earlier, soldiers based at Fort Dalles on the Miami River had kept warring Seminoles at bay, then supported federal blockaders' maneuvers along the South Florida coast. Writer Arva Moore Parks quotes one Union officer as describing those who remained in Miami after the Civil War as being "of all colors,

Cars first raced on Daytona Beach in 1902 and were still much in evidence in this photograph taken six years later. Automobiles are permitted on the tightly packed sand to this day.

Henry Flagler's grand Ponce de León Hotel rose in Saint Augustine in 1895. Its grand dining room is now the dining hall of Flagler College, which took over after the hotel's decline.

from Yankee to the ebony Congo, all armed, a more motley crew never trod Captain Kidd's ships . . . deserters from the Army and Navy of both sides, a mixture of Spanish and Cubans, outlaws and renegades." Years later many of the handful of permanent residents were black Bahamians, living in a settlement called Kebo and making a living off the spoils of wrecked ships. The city of Miami was not incorporated until 1896, when Flagler's railroad reached the area. Indeed, Miami is sometimes called "The City That Was Never a Town," for it sprang to city status almost magically. One of Flagler's great resort hotels, the Royal Palm, opened in 1897, and that same year the city began a tourism tradition by welcoming the International Tobacco Growers Association to town for a convention. By 1891 enough civilization had been carved from the wilderness that Flora McFarlane and five other women could found a Housekeepers' Club and begin raising money to build a new Sunday school building. One of the earliest mansions (now a museum) was the Barnacle, a bayfront house and boatyard built by Commodore Ralph Munroe. In the 1950s and '60s, the Grove became a hangout for hirsute artists, musicians, and other bohemians. Today, Coconut Grove is a fashionable center of groomed estates, resort hotels, chichi restaurants, CocoWalk shops, and pulsating nightclubs.

The 1920s brought the "Great Boom" to Miami, including the development of a planned "Mediterranean-theme" suburb called Coral Gables on an old grapefruit plantation. A terrible hurricane slowed the boom in 1926. It blew across the city with 125-mph winds, collapsing walls, tearing off roofs, driving ships aground, and killing dozens of people.

But 1926 was also the year that Pan American World Airways turned Miami into the "Gateway to the Americas" with flights from the city's Dinner Key—bringing waves of Latin tourists in return. Forty years later, after the arrival of a half-million Cuban exiles, Miami would call

The "Jewel Box Tea Party" in Tampa on October 19, 1923, was a splendid affair. The city was already more than thirty years into its reign as the gem of Florida's west coast.

itself the "Capital of Latin America." The 1980s and '90s saw the Miami skyline explode with new development, and the city's hosting of the 1994 Summit of the Americas confirmed the city's place among world political and financial centers. One of the old buildings to be refurbished was the Freedom Tower, built in 1924 as the city's first skyscraper. It later housed the offices of the *Miami News* and the processing center for thousands of Cuban refugees.

Miami Beach, whose array of small Art Deco hotels and gigantic apartment buildings and resort hotels has become a familiar South Florida landmark, was no more than a deserted barrier island, filled with thick mangroves and thicker waves of mosquitoes, until a Pennsylvania farmer, Henry B. Lum, bought thousands of acres on the beach from the state for thirty-five cents an acre in 1881. He envisioned a thriving coconut plantation, having seen the profusion of coconut palms that lined the ocean beach and the shoreline along Biscayne Bay. Other investors bought up land to the north of Lum's property, but everyone gave up the idea of harvesting coconuts when mosquitoes and sandflies drove their laborers out of the groves. One of the late-coming group of investors, John Collins of New Jersey, however, had some success growing "alligator pears"—avocados—farther up the beach. In the first decade of the new century, Collins, as well as brothers James and John Lummus—Miami bankers who had bought the old Lum plantation—hit upon the idea of turning what was then called Ocean Beach into a tourist resort on the Atlantic City model. They built bathhouses, oceanfront cottages, and bridges and started ferry service from the mainland. They drained mangrove swamps to eliminate mosquito breeding grounds, and the clatter of their dredgers drove off the alligator population. In 1915 Carl Fisher, an Indianian who had built the Indianapolis Motor Speedway in that state's capital, erected the Flamingo, the first grand Miami Beach hotel. A born promoter, Fisher bought a neon billboard at Fifth Avenue and Forty-second Street in New York and flashed, "It's June in Miami!" during the winter months. By 1921 there were five hotels and nine apartment houses on the beach. This was just the beginning, for the land boom of the following decade would turn nearly every inch of Miami Beach into a developed lot, and some real estate values multiplied one thousand times or more. During the beach's heyday, dozens of home and hotel owners, influenced by a modernist movement later called "Art Deco," painted their buildings in subtle pastels and "gemological" shades, including silver, jade, and emerald. Millionaires like Harvey Firestone decorated their Miami Beach estates, inside and out, in Egyptian, Aztec, Mexican, and Pueblo motifs, and in the 1930s, slashing "Zig-zag Moderne" symbols like electric flashes became fashionable in beachwear and architectural decor. By the time the craze subsided, more than eight hundred Miami Beach buildings had been decked out in Art Deco designs.

South Beach was one of the few resort areas in the nation open to Jews, and they settled there (and later in high-rise apartments up the beach) in great numbers. They built still more hotels, swelling Miami Beach's seasonal population to sixty thousand or more. Keith Root's *Art Deco Guide* to the Beach points out that half the beach's population was Jewish by 1947, but "Gentiles Only" signs were not outlawed until two years later. In the 1970s and '80s, Miami Beach went through a period of tawdry decline, and tourists turned to glitzier destinations in Florida and elsewhere. But a massive restoration and building boom followed in the 1990s, and the Beach again became a popular—and nostalgic—place to be and to be seen.

You won't find suburban sprawl very far west of Miami, however, for lapping at the city's edges are the vast and fragile Florida Everglades, only one-fifth of which are fully protected in Everglades National Park. The Everglades is not a swamp but rather an incredible, slow-moving, fifty-mile-wide "River of Grass," whose sweet water runs only six inches to three feet deep in most locations. The Everglades ecosystem, which gets its freshwater supply from rainfall and overflow from Lake Okeechobee is threatened on several fronts. Human manipulation of the release of water into the 'Glades during prolonged dry seasons kills snail populations and floods alligator nests. New species introduced by humans have killed off thousands of native plants and fish; the number of wading birds nesting in colonies in the southern Everglades alone declined 93 percent from the 1930s to the mid-1990s. And saltwater intrusion from man-made canals, plus pollution and agricultural runoff, have threatened other species. In response, the U.S. Congress extended the eastern boundary of Everglades National Park, which was created in 1947 to save the 'Glades. The message of Everglades preservationists is a simple one. It was succinctly sounded in 1947 by environmental visionary Marjory Stoneman Douglas, a Miami newspaperwoman: "There are no other Everglades in the world."

Tampa's Ybor City neighborhood lured the great cigarmaking factories from Key West—which in turn had snatched many cigar rollers away from Cuba during the Spanish-American War.

Descendants of the escaped Seminoles called the Miccosukee have lived in the Everglades since the middle of the nineteenth century. These people still keep a village along U.S. 41, called the Tamiami Trail, through the heart of the 'Glades. But not just Seminoles managed to find patches of dry ground on the edges of the Everglades. So, for thousands of years, did two other "People of the 'Glades": Tequestas to the east and Calusas to the south and west. Neither made use of metal or stone. They fashioned tools and utensils out of shells, and weapons out

of sticks and sharks' teeth. The Calusas fought the arriving Spanish bitterly, if futilely. An Indian arrow dipped in the extract of an indigenous plant superficially wounded Ponce de León, but the poison was so powerful that the explorer died several days later.

To the north of Miami, Broward County also extends into the Everglades, and its three hundred miles of navigable waterways have earned it the nickname "Venice of America." Judging by the boats that put into Fort Lauderdale, Pompano Beach, Hollywood, and other Broward oceanside towns, it may also be the yachting capital of the world. Broward is home to a Goodyear Blimp base, one of only four blimp headquarters in the world. In addition to its own beaches, glittering Las Olas Boulevard shopping district, and up-tempo "Strip" in Fort Lauderdale, the county offers 288 parks, three natural reefs, an artificial reef, and more than five hundred acres of Everglades.

A remarkable achievement of the U.S. Corps of Engineers, the Intracoastal Waterway, saving boaters from the pounding waves at sea, extends from Dade and Broward counties farther up the "Gold Coast" into Palm Beach County—and beyond, up the entire Eastern Seaboard. "Perfectly posh," one local magazine called the Palm Beaches. It "isn't just the color of money," reads the accompanying story. This former playground of the Flaglers, Rockefellers, Astors, and Fitzgeralds is "a saturated palette . . . [of] sensual and sultry pleasures." Palm Beach island is entered through a canopy of royal palms. Palm Beach, writes Arline Bleecker in the same article, is "a town so rarified it has no movie theater, no plumber, no electrician, not even an auto agency (despite the fact that it claims more Rolls-Royces per capita than London)." Worth Avenue is a Romanesque shopping district where one can browse among tasteful displays of ivory Foo dogs, white jade table screens, malachite vases, and eighteen-karat white-gold bracelets ringed with diamonds. The pampering continues at retreats like the 365-acre Boca Raton Resort & Club, in

The Hav-a-Tampa cigar factory was but one of dozens in the "Cigarmaking Capital of the World" in the 1920s, when cigars were as common a man's accessory as straw hats.

Thomas A. Edison donated more than two thousand palm trees to his winter hometown, Fort Myers, for planting along McGregor Boulevard. He had obtained the seedlings on a visit to Cuba.

south Palm Beach County, where the tennis is so serious, there's even a tennis concierge. West Palm Beach, once Palm Beach's scullery, caught the flow of the 1920s building boom, but also a later ebb that led to whole downtown neighborhoods of abandoned buildings. "West Palm" has come back to life with a vengeance, however, thanks to a new judicial center and courthouse, a new $60-million performing-arts center, and the infusion of trendy nightspots. Like Miami, the city is acquiring a growing Latin flavor, thanks to widespread immigration from Central and South America.

Farther up the coast, past the Kennedy Space Center complex, the people of Daytona Beach call the Intracoastal Waterway the "Halifax River," though it is no river at all. Auto racing was born in Daytona in 1902, when Alexander Winton and R. E. Olds raced on the beach. It's just one event recalled at the Birthplace of Speed Museum and at the city's annual antique car show and swap meet. Like Fort Lauderdale, Daytona Beach was long a favorite spring-break destination for frisky college students from northern states, which helps explain the assortment of gaudy hotels and scruffy souvenir shops along Highway A1A, the main road along the coastline and barrier islands. Farther north still, Saint Augustine retains some of the regal charm of its days as a Spanish colonial capital. There's the old Castillo de San Marcos fort, whose sixteen-foot-walls were built of coquina, a soft limestone made of shells, coral, and cement; the Spanish Quarter living-history village; the Lightner Museum in Henry Flagler's old Alacazar Hotel; Flagler College, whose centerpiece is the railroad baron's Ponce de León Hotel; and a tourist site dedicated to the questionable tale of a Fountain of Youth. It is not surprising that America's oldest city should also have several "oldest" attractions, including the "Oldest House" and the "Oldest Store Museum."

As antiquated as Saint Augustine is, Jacksonville to the north, near the state's northeastern corner on what natives call Florida's "First Coast," seems contrastingly new. The city, once named Cowford but renamed in honor of General Andrew Jackson in 1822, is a city of seemingly never-ending festivals, river regattas, footraces, fishing tournaments, nature-trail walks, and parades on its beaches and downtown Riverwalk. Sprawling Jacksonville, already one of the nation's largest cities in area, at 840 square miles, had grown to become the nation's sixteenth-largest city in population by the mid-1990s. One of the rewards, in 1995, was a new National Football League franchise, the Jaguars.

Off the *very* northeasternmost tip of Florida, a shell's skip from Georgia's barrier islands, lies Amelia Island, whose residents have lived under eight different flags in the island's four-hundred-year modern history. Birthplace of the nation's shrimping industry and a "rest stop" for 250 types of migratory birds on the "Eastern Flyway," Amelia Island includes a beach that was rated among the world's ten most beautiful by the television program *Lifestyles of the Rich and Famous.*

The drive across state to the capital, Tallahassee, in Florida's thin Panhandle, takes one past the southern edge of the Okefenokee Swamp, over the "Swanee" (Suwannee) River, through pine forests, and into Lake City—once called "Alligator" after a Seminole chief of that name. Old U.S. 90 then rolls over gentle red-clay hills and through small lumber and tobacco towns with wide, oak-shaded streets and white-columned houses. This was the heart of Confederate country, which tourists today mostly race past on Interstate 10. The state capital, Tallahassee, calls itself "Florida With a Southern Accent." There were once seventy-one plantations in the area, including one of the last to be built in the South. Though Union forces held Pensacola, farther west in the Panhandle, during the Civil War, and advanced on Tallahassee, they were rebuffed by a rag-tag force of boys and elderly men at the Battle of Natural Bridge, leaving Tallahassee the only Confederate capital east of the Mississippi to avoid capture. It became the center of state government after Florida's new territorial legislature met once in Saint Augustine, once in Pensacola, and decided to split the distance and set up permanently in Tallahassee. Old Tallahassee can be visualized today on a stroll past antebellum and turn-of-the-century homes along Park Avenue and Calhoun Street. The state's 1845 domed capitol still stands and is a favorite tourist attraction, but legislative business is now conducted at the newer, 307-foot-tall capitol. Dedicated in 1978, it was designed by Edward Durrell Stone, who also designed Washington, D.C.'s Kennedy Center for the Performing Arts. Fifteen miles south of the capital is Wakulla Springs, one of the world's deepest freshwater springs and an early Florida tourist attraction. Pensacola, the old capital of Spanish West Florida on the state's western border with Alabama, is so far west, it's in a different time zone—and almost eight hundred miles from Key West. That's almost the exact driving distance between New York and Chicago!

The hub of Florida's Gulf Coast is Tampa-Saint Petersburg, which is actually two quite distinct spheres of influence often in competition in matters such as attracting conventions and major-league sports franchises. Tampa offers world-class attractions like Busch Gardens Tampa Bay and the Florida Aquarium, spicy nightlife in Ybor City—the "SoHo of the South"—an innovative Museum of Science and

Thomas Edison and his wife, Mina, relax near their winter home. "There is only one Fort Myers," he said, "and ninety million people are going to find out about it."

Industry, and big-league hockey. Most of West Florida's oceangoing cruises depart out of Tampa's Garrison Seaport Center. It is Saint Petersburg, however, that offers the area's Gulf beaches, as do the smaller Tampa Bay communities of Bradenton and Sarasota. The latter was circus impresario John Ringling's chosen winter home. His palatial house and gardens are now the state art museum, anchored by his own fantastic collection of paintings, sculptures, and tapestries. The museum also includes a gallery of circus memorabilia from the showman's long career. And worth a visit a few miles north of the Bay is Tarpon Springs, still largely a Greek enclave from which divers set off for sponges that have finally returned more than four decades after a blight destroyed their offshore beds. And in nearby Citrus County, which calls itself "Mother Nature's Theme Park," the world's largest herd of wintering manatees—sea cows often mistaken for mermaids by early mariners—can be seen in the wild or at Homosassa Springs State Wildlife Park.

Southwest Florida, anchored by Fort Myers and Naples, has had its millionaire snowbirds as well. Thomas Edison and Henry Ford wintered in Fort Myers on the Caloosahatchee River. Their homes, and Edison's workshop and experimental botanical gardens, are now city-owned attractions. Lee County beaches have been ranked third-best in the world for shelling, the western gateway to the Everglades beckons nearby, and tarpon fishing—which originated in Pine Island Sound—is still serious sport along the "Lee Island Coast." It's little wonder the area calls itself "Florida's Florida."

Where in 1924 serene orange groves (right) stood near Orlando are now acres of entertainment theme parks, housing subdivisions, skyscrapers, and business parks. The event that changed the face of the once-sleepy cattle and citrus town forever was the opening of Disney's Magic Kingdom, captured (opposite) by the Orlando Sentinel *in 1971.*

Up in the state's central interior lies Orlando, founded by U.S. soldiers who had fought the elusive Seminoles and stayed to form a community named for Orlando Reeves, a soldier who was killed by an Indian arrow while on sentinel duty. Orlando was transformed from a virtual cowtown and citrus shipping center to perhaps the world's best-known constellation of family theme parks. The 1939 Federal Writers Program *Guide to Florida* noted that "sidewalks are narrow; traffic signal lights bear the admonition 'Quiet.'" Today joyful noise is the rule at Sea World of Florida—the world's largest zoological park—Universal Studios Florida, Cypress Gardens, the ever-expanding Walt Disney World, and smaller attractions like Silver Springs, Gatorland, and Shell World. Cypress Gardens predated the Magic Kingdom, but it was Disney's clandestine purchase of twenty-eight thousand acres in the late 1960s that changed the character of Orlando forever. Once the Epcot Center "community of tomorrow," and an MGM-Disney Studios theme park, were added to the Disney Empire, Orlando was golden as a family vacation destination, international airline port of call, and invigorated business center. Problem is, many of the area's sites are worth a day or more's visit apiece, which, taken together, can mean more time, money, and patience than parents can afford. In fact, Orlando tourism officials have estimated that a family would need *forty-five days* to fully enjoy all of the area's attractions. So, difficult choices must be made.

Sunny. Lush. Aqua. Orange. Neon. Balmy. Sweet. Ancient. Ultramodern. Multicultural. Florida offers a kaleidoscope of images not soon forgotten.

OVERLEAF: One can almost feel Miami's vibrancy in its shimmering nighttime skyline. Yet it was barely a century ago that Henry Flagler carved a settlement out of a dense subtropical wilderness. "Boomtown U.S.A." in the 1920s, this polyglot international business capital exploded again in the 1990s with new skyscrapers, sports teams, and restaurants.

The pace of life quickly turns carefree south of Miami, in the Florida Keys. At Islamorada at mile marker 82.7 in the Upper Keys, carver Dick Thomas displays his creations (left), hewn from cypress, at the Tiki & Company roadside stand. Sea shells of all descriptions can be found along the long, narrow road to Key West as well. On many days, thousands of tourists get their photos snapped at the "southernmost" point in the continental United States (above) in Key West. Truth be told, the actual point is across the way on a military base. The nation's southernmost point overall can be found on a Hawaiian island.

Nobel Prize-winning author Ernest Hemingway wrote eight of his most famous novels, notably A Farewell to Arms and For Whom the Bell Tolls, at his Spanish Colonial-style home in Key West (right). Hemingway kept nearly fifty cats—including several six-toed varieties—on the grounds, and some of their direct descendants still loll about. Also on the key, in the courtyard of a Civil War fort called West Martello Tower, are the lush plantings of the Key West Garden Club (opposite)— one of the island's last free tourist attractions. The fort, which was captured by federal troops, is highlighted by vaulted ceilings, gun mounts, and a conservatory. The botanical gardens feature rare native, exotic, and tropical specimens, an exhaustive catalogue of which is available at the door.

Key West's old Strand Theater (opposite) is now the home of Ripley's Believe It or Not "odditorium." Sloppy Joe's Bar (top left), where the sandwich of the same name is said to have originated, was Ernest Hemingway's favorite watering hole. It changed locations in 1933 after the landlord raised the rent from $3.75 to more than $5 a month. The proprietors now spend hundreds of times that much each month. President Truman kept a winter retreat at the "Little White House" (bottom left) on the grounds of a military barracks in Key West's Old Town. The neighborhood has been developed into an eclectic mix of condominiums and family homes. The pier owned by the Edgewater Lodge on Long Key (overleaf) becomes a virtual bird sanctuary when conditions turn windy.

Even the outdoor art has a nautical theme (opposite) outside the Italian Fisherman Restaurant along U.S. Highway 1 in Key Largo. Egrets (above) are one species cared for at the Florida Keys Wild Bird Center on Tavernier Island in the Keys. Wild birds have suffered as the human population encroaches upon their habitat. The center's wildlife rehabilitators care for injured birds who have collided with vehicles, power lines, or windows; have become entangled in monofilament fish lines; or have swallowed baited hooks. Visitors often ask why many of the herons, roseat spoonbills, pelicans, and other birds are caged in large enclosures. It's because the creatures often arrive suffering and emaciated. Once their progress has been monitored and they have recovered, they are released into the wild. When hurricanes strike the Keys, staff and volunteers take the birds inside—often into their own homes!

In 1982, Jim and Frankie Hendricks bought the African Queen *(above)*—the boat featured in the classic 1951 Humphrey Bogart-Katherine Hepburn movie. They moved it to Key Largo harbor, where they own a Holiday Inn. The boat, built in 1912 in England, served as an actual African steamer. The Hendrickses found it blistering in a cow pasture near Ocala, Florida. Sunset's many hues at the Marathon Marina *(right)* delight strollers on Marathon Key. The Everglades' slowly moving "River of Grass" *(overleaf)*, more than one hundred miles wide, eventually drains into Florida Bay. There are scattered dry spots, called "hammocks," on which deer, bears, and an occasional cougar can be spotted.

Alligators are not to be trifled with in the Everglades (left), where they abound. The gator uses camouflage—its remarkable resemblance to a floating log—to glide close to unsuspecting prey. Small game—and even an occasional deer, cow, or human—will wander too close to the water's edge and be pounced upon by the beasts, who look ponderous but can rush out of the water with remarkable quickness. The thrashing alligator will then twist and drown its terrified victims. Once an officially endangered species, the gators have made such a comeback that they are straying into residential canals and yards. Few Florida palm trees are harvested in the wild. They are carefully cultivated in irrigated fields like the High Hopes Nursery's spread (above) south of Miami.

Coral Castle (above) in Homestead was a remarkable example of love turned to stone. Jilted on the eve of his wedding, Edward Leedskalnin became reclusive. Over twenty-five years, using only handmade tools, this five-foot-tall, one-hundred-pound Latvian native somehow moved more than eleven hundred tons of coral rock several miles, then sculpted and carved them into a remarkable series of stone tributes to the girl he called his "Sweet Sixteen."

A rare white Bengal tiger (right) roams beyond a moat at Miami's Metrozoo. One of three whites in the zoo's Temple exhibit, the animal is not an albino; it has blue eyes and a rare lack of normal orange pigmentation. Almost one thousand animals of 250 or more species roam the zoo's 290-acre habitat.

Hundreds of parrots (above), cockateels, and other chattery, brightly plumed mimics star in four daily shows at Parrot Jungle and Gardens, southwest of Miami. Visitors can also get a close-up view of reptiles, small mammals, birds of prey, and more than twelve hundred varieties of exotic plants. There's a flamingo preserve there—and also at the Miami Metrozoo (left). In South Miami, too, the spectacular Vizcaya Gardens (overleaf) were a playground in the sun on the grounds of the winter retreat of James Deering, co-founder of the International Harvester Company. The gardens and majestic Italianate mansion at the edge of Biscayne Bay are now a museum.

A classical colonnade around a halcyon pool (left) frames the gardens of the Vizcaya Museum. Diego Suarez, a Colombian born architect trained in France, designed the gardens. At the time of the estate's construction between 1914 and 1916 Miami's population was around ten thousand. More than one thousand workers labored on the Vizcaya project. The government of Spain donated the statue of Juan Ponce de León, in downtown Miami, for the 1976 U.S. Bicentennial. The explorer, who arrived on the peninsula on Easter Sunday 1513 and named it "Florida," died of a wound received in the Florida Keys from an Indian arrow tipped in the juices of a deadly tree.

Little Havana (right), along Calle Ocho— Eighth Street—is a colorful neighborhood of markets, shops, and parks. Two waves of Cuban immigrants settled in the Miami district, where there are now statues to heroes of Cuban independence, a "sidewalk of stars" similar to Hollywood's Walk of Fame, innumerable Spanish signs, and restaurants serving delicacies like fried Cuban sandwiches. CocoWalk (above) is a collage of stylish fashion and food establishments in the heart of Miami's oldest neighborhood— Coconut Grove. By the time Miami became a city in 1896, Cocoanut Grove, settled by Bahamian immigrants, was already thriving. In 1919 it dropped the "a" from its name. Influenced by nearby Caribbean cultures, many South Miami villas like this one (overleaf) sport bright colors and trademark tile roofs.

Because more than five hundred thousand Cuban refugees registered at a processing center in Miami's first skyscraper (above) in the 1960s, the structure became known as "Freedom Tower." The 1924 landmark, which housed the offices of the Miami News, was extensively renovated in the mid-1990s. The view from the top floors of the First Union Bank Building (right), overlooking the Miami River, is nothing short of spectacular. There are more skyscrapers across the river in the Brickell area of downtown. Although Miami's gleaming skyscrapers give a first impression of another sterile glass-and-steel urban canyon, the city below is alive with activity—in dozens of languages. Miami is the undisputed financial and trading gateway to all the Americas, but its banks, malls, and commercial-district shops represent cultures—and cater to customers—from around the world.

CHINA GRILL

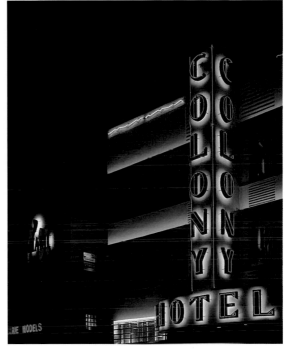

Miami's Metromover light-rail system (opposite) has two overhead loops through downtown and extensions north and south across the city. The China Grill (left) and the Colony Hotel (above) are glowing proof that, at night, Miami Beach's South Beach is a sea of neon. The 1935 Colony Hotel, on Ocean Avenue, falls within the city's historic district, so the building's illumination must respect the original design, when neon was more of an accent than a prominent feature. The newer round restaurant and office tower stands outside the district, so, like a Times Square or Las Vegas building, it is free to spiral its neon up the entire building.

South Beach (opposite and above) has one of the world's largest concentrations of Art Deco buildings, which make a fascinating architectural statement, daytime or at night and with or without neon accent. The Art Deco name derives from the 1925 Exposition International des Arts Decoratifs et Industriels Modernes in Paris, which introduced novel combinations of Pre-Columbian, Cubist, "machine Expressionist," and even "Zig Zag Moderne" styles. Sharp corners, sparse fixtures, electric embellishments, and pastel shades were some of the features admired and emulated by the captains of commerce who developed Miami Beach. Northward from South Beach (overleaf), Miami Beach is lined with condominiums, modern hotel towers, and rental apartments. With the development of even swankier resort communities farther up the Florida Coast, Miami Beach suffered a precipitous decline. Extensively renovated, it has since bounced back to again become a favorite haunt of the world's "beautiful people."

Temple Emanu-El (opposite), on Washington Avenue in Miami Beach, was built in 1947, at the height of the influx of Jewish property owners and beachgoers. The beach was one of the few in the nation open to Jews, and Keith Root, in his superb Art Deco Guide *to Miami Beach, notes that many Jewish investors who had gone south for health reasons filled their "semi-retirement" by building and operating small apartment houses. Not all Miami Beach towers are vintage structures that have—or have not—been refurbished. In an exclusive neighborhood known as "South of Fifth," South Beach's tallest building, the forty-four-story Portofino Tower condominium and resort (left) rose in the mid-1990s. It offers a panoramic view up the beach theretofore available only from a helicopter.*

The Jackie Gleason Theater of the Performing Arts (above), named for the legendary impresario who produced his television show in the building, is located next door to Miami Beach's convention center. Broadway shows, performances by the Miami City Ballet and the Florida Philharmonic Orchestra, shows by entertainers like magician David Copperfield, and reviews by the theater's own resident dance company fill a busy year-round season. It requires a double-take to be certain the "view" through the archway at the ornate Fountainebleau Hilton Resort and Towers on Collins Avenue is an illusion, the work of a crafty muralist. Like a few other luxury hotels on Florida's beaches of Florida, the Fountainebleau offers lavish pools (two, in fact: a saltwater pool and a one-half-acre "heated lagoon").

Roy Lichtenstein created the sculpture (top right) in front of the Miami Beach Convention Center—Dade County's largest convention facility. In 1930, architect Russell Pancoast, grandson of Miami Beach pioneer John A. Collins, designed the Miami Beach Library and Art Center. Thirty-four years later, philanthropists John and Johanna Bass offered the center their multi-million-dollar art collection, along with funds to expand the facility to house two prized tapestries. When the work was completed, the facility's name was changed to the Bass Museum of Art. The bronze at the museum entrance, executed in 1958, is Chaim Gross's Happy Mother (bottom right). Kenneth Triester created the Sculpture of Love and Anguish (opposite) at the Holocaust Memorial in Miami Beach. He describes it as "a scene from hell . . . frozen in painted bronze."

64

Fort Lauderdale (opposite) is a shining Florida success story. Long a scruffy collegiate "Spring Break" destination, the city has revitalized its world-class beach with a wave-shaped promenade wall and walkway, trimmed with tempting cafés. A spectacular performing-arts center capped its cultural renaissance. Up the coast in Palm Beach, Worth Avenue (left) remains one of America's poshest shopping destinations. The Boca Raton Resort & Club (above), founded as the Cloister Inn in 1926, typifies the elegance of that seaside resort. Its "Boca pink," now a recognized color, is designed to represent the "perfect sunset." The Breakers (overleaf) in Palm Beach has also been one of the "Gold Coast's" favorite wintertime addresses of socialites and celebrities.

Beverly Hills has its Rodeo Drive, New York its Fifth Avenue, and the newest of the world's chic shopping promenades is Fort Lauderdale's Las Olas Boulevard (opposite). Anchored by the restored Riverside Hotel, Las Olas ("The Waves" in Spanish) is lined with boutiques, art galleries, restaurants and sidewalk cafés, and jazz houses. The Cluett Memorial Gardens (above) are a languid setting outside Palm Beach's Church of Bethesda-by-the-Sea. The Episcopal church gets its name from the biblical story of Christ's healing at the Pool of Bethesda. America's oldest city gate (overleaf), not unexpectedly, can be seen in the nation's oldest city—Saint Augustine—founded in 1565. The gate was part of the defensive wall that protected the city from attack. It, and much of the restored area to which it opens, is now maintained by the National Park Service.

Saint Augustine is a history-lover's paradise. Inside the oldest surviving Spanish colonial structure, the Gonzáles-Alvarez House (above) is a museum whose exhibits cover the more than four centuries of history of the old colonial outpost. The site has been continuously occupied by Europeans or Americans since the early 1600s. Restored historic buildings— including America's oldest wooden schoolhouse in the foreground—front Saint George Street (right) along the old Spanish Quarter. The cedar and cypress school building was constructed during the second Spanish period, from 1784 to 1821. Railroad baron Henry Flagler built more than fifteen magnificent structures in America's "Southern Newport," including Presbyterian, Baptist, and Methodist churches. But his crowning achievement was the Ponce de León Hotel (overleaf), now owned by Flagler College.

Bustling Jacksonville (left), on Florida's northeast "First Coast," is known for its festive, and mostly free, festivals, including those for kite, powerboating, pier-fishing, and sand-castle-building enthusiasts. The Mug Race sailboat regatta on the Saint Johns River is, at forty-two miles, the longest in the world. Jacksonville became a major-league sports city with the arrival of a National Football League team in 1995.

A likeness of its Jaguar mascot (above) menaces outside Memorial Stadium. Idyllic dunes (overleaf) dot remote reaches that share Amelia Island with fabulous resorts, elegant hotels, and Fernandina Beach—the historic border port between Spanish Florida and English or American territory. Eight flags—including those of pirates, French Huguenots, and the southern Confederacy—have flown over the island.

Florida confronts its sometimes-racist history forthrightly. The stories of both dreadful and positive episodes in the state's African-American history—from Ku Klux Klan atrocities and demeaning products and minstrel shows, to achievements by war heroes and statesmen— are recounted at the state's Black Archives (above) in Tallahassee's old Freedman's (later Union) Bank. For example, U.S. Supreme Court Justice Thurgood Marshall's life's story is told in detail at the archive. Many of the city's pioneers, their slaves, and white and black Civil War troops from both sides—Tallahassee was the only southern capital never captured by Union forces—are buried in Old City Cemetery (right).

Florida's state government is quartered in a nondescript office tower. The adjacent Old State Capitol (opposite), built in 1845, has been restored to its 1902 appearance, with red candy-striped awnings, stained-glass dome, and classic rotunda. When there was talk of demolishing the landmark in the 1970s, opponents successfully fought the measure; the building is now a museum of Florida's political history. A walk around the lake in the Panhandle town of DeFuniak Springs is a stroll into Victoriana, when grand homes incorporated elaborate architectural details. Pictured (above) are painstakingly restored houses on Circle Drive. DeFuniak Springs was a winter headquarters of the New York Chautauqua movement. From 1885 to 1922, thousands of visitors traveled there for "instruction, recreation, amusement, fellowship, elocution, philosophy, and cookery." DeFuniak's Chautauqua is still celebrated, beginning with Illumination Night in February and continuing through a Chautauqua Festival in April.

North Florida—or the "real Florida," as natives like to call it—has long had the geography and genteel pace of the Old South. Its piney woods match those found from North Carolina to Louisiana. At Falling Waters Recreation Area, near Chipley in the Panhandle (above), visitors can picnic, hike, and see falls that descend into a one-hundred-foot-deep sinkhole in the woods. Because yellow pines grow quickly, many nearby landowners are converting former farmland into tree farms. In the Panhandle town of Wausau, residents have erected a monument to—of all things—the lowly possum (opposite). At the extreme western tip of the Panhandle, Pensacola is a city of beautiful churches, including Christ Episcopal (overleaf). Anglican presence in Florida dates from 1764, when the Bishop of London dispatched a missionary priest there. The Spanish Renaissance-style building was completed in 1903.

ERECTED IN GRATEFUL RECOGNITION OF THE ROLE THE NORTH AMERICAN POSSUM, A MAGNIFICIENT SURVIVOR OF THE MARSUPIAL FAMILY PRE-DATING THE AGES OF THE MASTADON AND THE DINOSAUR, HAS PLAYED IN FURNISHING BOTH FOOD AND FUR FOR THE EARLY SETTLERS AND THEIR SUCCESSORS. THEIR PRESENCE HERE HAS PROVIDED A SOURCE OF NUTRITIOUS AND FLAVORFUL FOOD IN NORMAL TIMES AND HAS BEEN IMPORTANT AID TO HUMAN SURVIVAL IN TIMES OF DISTRESS AND CRITICAL NEED.

THE 1982 SESSION OF THE FLORIDA LEGISLATURE FURTHER RECOGNIZED THE POSSUM BY PASSING A JOINT RESOLUTION PROCLAIMING THE FIRST SATURDAY IN AUGUST AS POSSUM DAY IN THE GREAT STATE OF FLORIDA.

ERECTED
BY
WAUSAU COMMUNITY DEVELOPMENT CLUB
AUG. 7, 1982

DESIGNED AND ERECTED BY:
SAPP MEMORIAL, INC.
COTTONDALE FLA

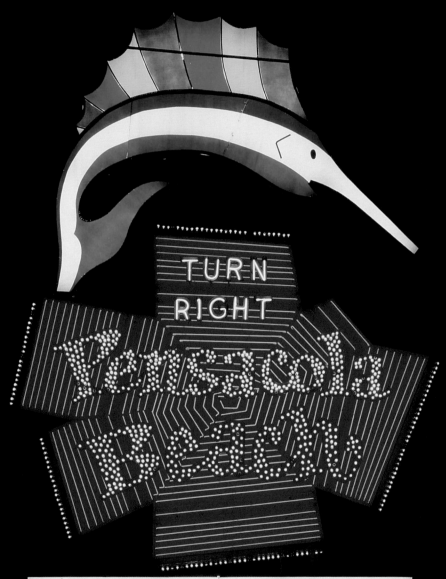

TURN
RIGHT

Pensacola
Beach

SCENIC DRIVE EAST ALONG
GULF OF MEXICO

's Whitest Beaches
S • RESTAURANTS

After a long drive, the sign to Pensacola Beach (opposite) is a welcome sight, especially to sun-lovers in nearby Louisiana, Mississippi, and Alabama, where beaches are either nonexistent or less beautiful than the white sands of the western tip of Florida. Annie and Mary Ella "Sunshine" Gibson bought the 1907 Franklin Hotel in Apalachicola, in the Florida Panhandle, in 1923 and lent the cypress-and-pine inn their last name. With its two decks of wrap-around porches, wicker chairs, and tin roof, the Gibson Inn (top left), now restored, exudes tropical indolence. Stories are served with the margaritas at the Gibson Bar (bottom left). When Hurricane Kate devastated Apalachicola in November 1985, owner Michael Koun brazenly tossed a candlelight "hurricane party" in the bar.

Tampa (right) is Florida's third-largest city, behind Miami and Jacksonville, but it is the second-largest employment center. Its port is the nation's eleventh-largest in cargo tonnage (first in Florida), and its airport is consistently rated tops in America by the Airline Passengers Association. The dock in the foreground accommodates water taxis that ply the Hillsborough River. Like Henry Flagler on Florida's east coast, Henry Plant built the railroad that opened the west coast to development. Plant, too, erected luxurious hotels to accommodate wealthy "snowbirds." His jewel was the onion-domed, five-hundred-room Tampa Bay Hotel in Tampa (opposite), built in 1891. The strange architectural concoction—mixing Victorian, Spanish, and Moorish elements, is now the main building of the University of Tampa.

CERAMICA STA ANA
SEVILLA (TRIANA) SPAIN

Ybor City is historic cigarmaking district. But today, with its lively clubs, galleries, and brewpub, it's more like the SoHo of the South. On Ybor's Seventh Avenue is the hand-tiled façade of the Columbia Restaurant (opposite). The intricate decoration stretches around the block. Carmela Varsalona (above) began wrapping cigars in factories as a sixteen-year-old. In her prime, she could produce four hundred hand-rolled cigars a day. The process involves rolling a rough bunch of filler leaves, then squeezing them into a press to obtain the cigar's distinctive shape. Next, the hand-rolled cigar is wrapped in a select outer leaf and snipped. Ideally, a fine cigar then ages a month or more to reduce the moisture in the tobacco leaves. Mrs. Varsalona now helps her grandson, Jim Tyre, roll cigars for his Cammorata cigar shop in Tampa's Urban Center.

Visitors to the Florida Aquarium on Tampa's waterfront get a rare view of hatchling alligators (above)—not lounging on a shoreline or floating like a sinister log, but swimming freely in front of them. Interactive programs feature scuba divers and aquatic educators. Inside the aquarium's dome are more than fifty-three hundred animals and plants, including cypress trees, native to the state. In the offshore exhibit, brown sharks and a jewfish weighing more than one hundred pounds swim together. The gators are full-grown and menacing at Busch Gardens Tampa Bay (right). The 335-acre park has nine theme areas, including "Egypt," which features the world's longest and tallest inverted roller coaster, "Montu." It slings riders at speeds exceeding sixty miles an hour.

Until synthetic sponges were developed, sponge diving thrived in the Greek-American village of Tarpon Springs, north of Tampa. A few sponge boats (above) still head out to gather the porous invertebrates. Then the catch is brought to shore for drying and display. On a building in town is a mural (opposite) dedicated to John Cocoris, who founded Tarpon Springs's sponge-diving industry in 1905. About the same time in Saint Petersburg, a plumbing contractor, George Turner, purchased a home along a dirt road north of town and discovered a large sinkhole and a shallow lake on the property. An avid horticulturist, Turner lined the lake with drainage tile, then turned it and the sinkhole into habitats for exotic plants. Visits to his gardens became a Suncoast tradition for which the enterprising Turner charged a nickel. Today Sunken Gardens (overleaf) is Florida's oldest family-owned attraction.

Florida's alligators are the reluctant stars of gator-wrestling shows in parks around the state. At Sunken Gardens in Saint Petersburg, muscular Paul Strazzula (opposite) corners a beast, grabs it by the tail, pushes down its snout to keep it from chomping him, clamps his hand around its jaw, and lifts the 220-pound creature for all to see. Strazzula notes that the alligator's brain-power is so dim that, no matter how many times he wrestles a particular gator, it does not recognize him. Each show, it thinks he's a new predator—and reacts accordingly. The stunning Sunshine Skyway (top left) over Tampa Bay connects Saint Petersburg and Bradenton. Beautiful Saint Petersburg Harbor (bottom left) is a favorite docking point for cruise ships bound for Mexico and Gulf islands.

John Ringling, the youngest of seven Ringling Brothers, and his wife, Mable, settled in Sarasota, where the brothers' circus wintered. Ringling collected art on a grand scale and built a museum next to his home in which to display it. In the courtyard (opposite), are beautiful columns, fountains, and statues, including a bronze cast of Michelangelo's David (right), the only one in the western world. The Ringlings did not emphasize their circus connection, but the State of Florida, to which the Ringlings bequeathed their Sarasota property, opened a circus gallery. It is loaded with circus costumes, photographs, and other memorabilia. Pictured (overleaf) are a replica 1902 griffin wagon made by Ringling employees and, to the right, a 1920 thirty-three-whistle calliope wagon used by the Sells-Floto Circus.

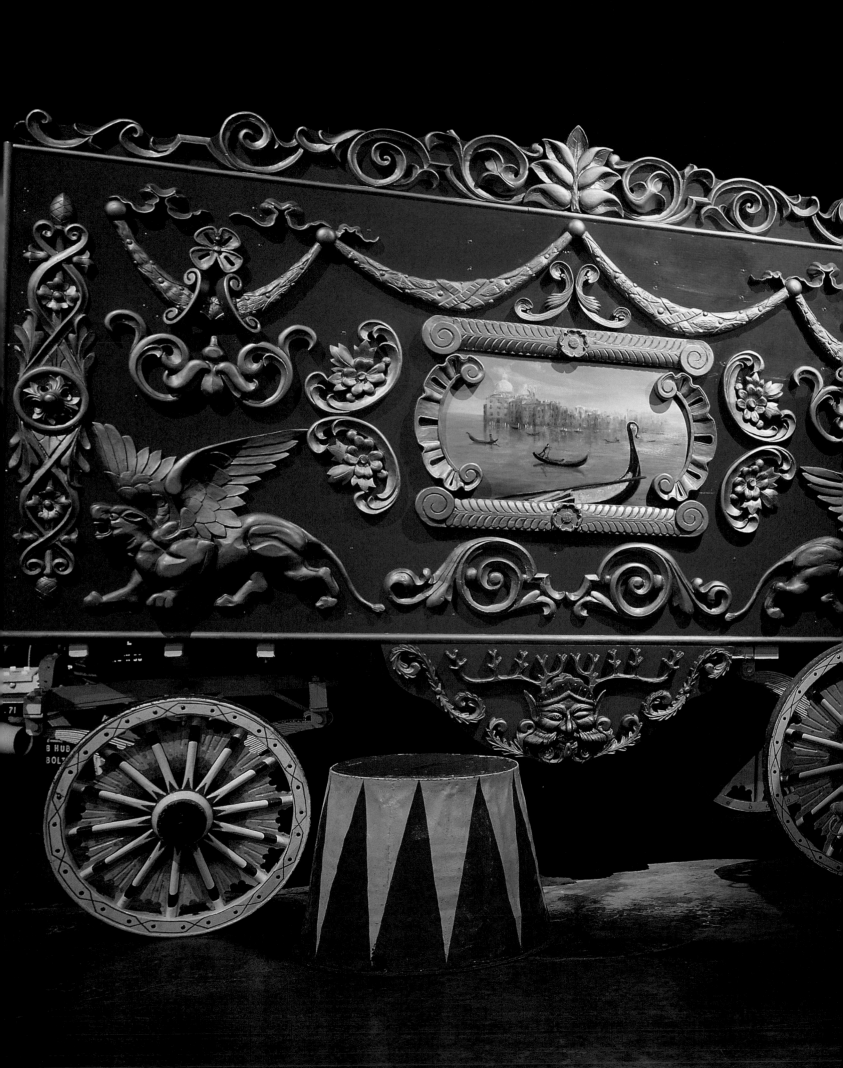

Florida is packed with eclectic attractions, including the Teddy Bear Museum in Naples, where bears are even a part of the outdoor statuary (above). It was opened in 1990 after "Frannie" Pew Hayes, an inveterate traveler and arctophile (teddy-bear lover), assembled more than three thousand stuffed and mechanical bears and "bearaphernalia" like bear books and jewelry. The area east of Naples, near the Everglades, is rapidly developing. The Freedom Horses display (right), dedicated in 1992, can be found at the entrance to the Lely Resort Golf and Country Club. Sculptress Veryl Goodnight fabricated each of the one-ton, "life-and-a-quarter-size" bronze horses in Joseph, Oregon. One of her models was Rising Star, the horse that Robert Redford rode in the movie The Electric Horseman.

Not everything is old in the historic Olde Naples section of that luxurious Southwest Florida city. Streets are lined with magnificent contemporary homes (left). In Fort Myers are the winter homes of inventor Thomas Edison and industrialist Henry Ford. Ford brought his chief engineer, Frank Campbell, to Fort Myers and on most of his world travels, so the two could collaborate on new ideas. Campbell worked at the drafting board on the porch of the home (above), which Ford bought in 1916. On that porch, the Fords and Edisons often discussed nature, their current projects, and world events with their friends, including rubber baron Harvey Firestone and naturalist John Burroughs.

111

Thomas Alva Edison, the man of 1,093 patented inventions, maintained a winter home, "Seminole Lodge," in Fort Myers. In 1928, he set up a laboratory (top and bottom, right), where his work departed from his electronic tinkering in New Jersey. He was trying to perfect a new kind of rubber to circumvent the world monopoly on natural rubber. Edison produced rubber from goldenrod flowers, but in quantities too limited for mass production. Outside the lab is a gigantic banyan tree— Ficusbenghalensis— (opposite) with its classic aerial roots. The tree, which Harvey Firestone presented to Edison after a trip to India, measures more than four hundred feet in circumference. Near Winter Haven, southern belles, beautiful birds, and spectacular floral displays greet visitors at Cypress Gardens (overleaf), Florida's first theme park.

Cypress groves more spectacular than many in the Everglades have been carefully cultivated at Cypress Gardens (opposite) in Polk County. Nearby Lake Wales is known as the "City of Bells," thanks to one of the world's great carillons inside the Bok Tower (left). The fifty-seven bronze bells, which are played in concert each afternoon, range from seventeen pounds to nearly twelve tons. The tower and surrounding gardens were created by Edward Bok, a Dutch immigrant and editor of the Ladies Home Journal. He hired landscape architect Frederick Law Olmsted Jr. to turn a sandhill into a tropical garden. With President Calvin Coolidge presiding, the complex was dedicated to the American people in 1929. The area of Central Florida around Kissimmee and Saint Cloud is world-renowned orange country (overleaf).

Palm trees are a classic Florida symbol, and in mushrooming Orlando, the palms outside the Peabody Hotel sparkle at night (opposite) year-round. Orlando's Universal Studios Florida (above) is a working motion-picture and television studio and theme park. Its characters, including Frankenstein, Woody Woodpecker, Rocky and Bullwinkle, Yogi Bear and Scooby Doo, and E. T. derive from Universal's film and television characters. So do its rides—including "Back to the Future" and "Earthquake"—and its live shows, taken from The Wild, Wild West; The Blues Brothers; Terminator 2; and other Universal productions. The theme park's most famous ride brings visitors into close contact with a thirty-two-foot, three-ton, animated "Jaws" great white shark. Wandering the sets are celebrity look-alikes modeled on W. C. Fields, the Marx Brothers, Popeye, Mae West, Stan Laurel and Oliver Hardy, Charlie Chaplin, and others.

The talents of set designers are showcased at Universal Studios Florida. The "New York Public Library" (left) is actually an artfully decorated "matte painting." "Lombard's Landing" and "Fisherman's Cove" (above) are not in San Francisco, but are firmly entrenched on a Universal Studios lagoon on which speed-boat exhibitions thrill spectators. Universal Studios has nine full-time, working sound stages. The cable-TV network Nickelodeon produces many of its programs on one of them. Sea World of Florida (overleaf) down the road, is the world's most popular marinelife park. It features shows, rides, and exhibits of polar bears, whales, manatees, sea lions, penguins, dolphins, sharks, and more. Orlando has so many attractions that a family could not see them all in even the best-planned vacation.

123

At Sea World of Florida, Virgil Pelican (opposite) delights children and amateur photographers with his flapping dances and other antics. Shamu the Whale is the park's big draw, but playful dolphins (above) entertain visitors as well. These bottlenose dolphins, which humans came to adore through the Flipper *movies and* Jacques Cousteau's *epic underwater pho-* tography, chatter among themselves. The sound is picked up by underwater microphones and broadcast to Sea World visitors. The sounds serve as com- munication, but the mammals also read the echo from each other's calls to help locate objects in the water. Like whales, dolphins have blow- holes, out of which they spew excess water when they surface to take deep breaths. These intelligent crea- tures will lead fish away from trawlers' nets. In captivity they will jump in forma- tion, blow bubbles, and allow children to nuzzle their foreheads.

Index

The sun sets spectacularly, as is its habit in Florida, over the palms that surround the Ritz-Carlton resort on Amelia Island, near the Georgia line.

When civilization did finally push through the state's sawgrass and swamps, the hotels and resorts that resulted were among the world's most sumptuous.